JAN      2014

W9-BEF-102

# SCIENCE KIDS
## Life Cycles

# Plants

**Aaron Carr**

www.av2books.com

LET'S READ

AV²
BY WEIGL™

ADDED VALUE • AUDIO VISUAL

Go to **www.av2books.com**,
and enter this book's
unique code.

## BOOK CODE

**Q72538**

**AV² by Weigl** brings you media
enhanced books that support
active learning.

AV² provides enriched content that supplements and complements this book. Weigl's AV² books strive to create inspired learning and engage young minds in a total learning experience.

# Your AV² Media Enhanced books come alive with...

**Audio**
Listen to sections of
the book read aloud.

**Video**
Watch informative
video clips.

**Embedded Weblinks**
Gain additional information
for research.

**Try This!**
Complete activities and
hands-on experiments.

**Key Words**
Study vocabulary, and
complete a matching
word activity.

**Quizzes**
Test your knowledge.

**Slide Show**
View images and
captions, and prepare
a presentation.

# ... and much, much more!

Published by AV² by Weigl
350 5th Avenue, 59th Floor  New York, NY  10118
Website: www.av2books.com    www.weigl.com

Library of Congress Control Number: 2013934640
ISBN 978-1-62127-492-6 (hardcover)
ISBN 978-1-62127-498-8 (softcover)

Printed in the United States of America in North Mankato, Minnesota
2 3 4 5 6 7 8 9 0  17 16 15 14 13

092013
WEP100913

Senior Editor: Aaron Carr
Art Director: Terry Paulhus

Weigl acknowledges Getty Images as the primary image supplier for this title.

**2**

# Plants

# CONTENTS

**4**

All plants begin life, grow,
and make more plants.
This is a life cycle.

Plants begin life as seeds. Seeds need plenty of water. This helps them grow into healthy plants.

7

Seedlings need both sunlight and water to grow. The stem grows taller and the roots grow longer.

Leaves also start to grow from the stem.

Plants use sunlight to make their food. They can not live without the Sun.

The more sunlight a plant gets, the bigger it may grow.

13

Over time, the seedling grows into a fully grown plant. Most plants have flowers when they are fully grown. The plant is now ready to make new plants.

Plants make seeds when they flower. Plants spread their seeds to make new plants. Then, the life cycle starts over again.

Some plants spread their seeds in the wind.

Every plant has its own traits. These can be size, color, or shape. Plants pass on their traits through their seeds. This is why a seed from a tulip will grow into another tulip.

20

A life cycle can be different for different plants. Some plants complete the life cycle in one year. Others take two or more years to finish a life cycle.

# Life Cycles Quiz

Test your knowledge of plant life cycles by taking this quiz. Look at these pictures. Which stage of the life cycle do you see in each picture?

# KEY WORDS

Research has shown that as much as 65 percent of all written material published in English is made up of 300 words. These 300 words cannot be taught using pictures or learned by sounding them out. They must be recognized by sight. This book contains 67 common sight words to help young readers improve their reading fluency and comprehension. This book also teaches young readers several important content words, such as proper nouns. These words are paired with pictures to aid in learning and improve understanding.

| Page | Sight Words First Appearance |
|------|------------------------------|
| 5 | a, all, and, grow, is, life, make, more, plants, this |
| 6 | as, helps, into, need, of, them, water |
| 9 | after, few, it, kinds, may, one, or, other, some, take, to, two, when |
| 11 | also, both, from, the |
| 12 | can, food, gets, live, not, their, they, use, without |
| 15 | are, have, most, new, now, over, time |
| 16 | again, in, then |
| 18 | another, be, every, has, its, on, own, these, through, why, will |
| 21 | different, for, year |

| Page | Content Words First Appearance |
|------|--------------------------------|
| 5 | life cycle |
| 6 | seeds |
| 9 | months, seedling, weeks |
| 11 | leaves, roots, stem, sunlight |
| 12 | Sun |
| 15 | flowers |
| 16 | wind |
| 18 | color, shape, size, traits, tulip |

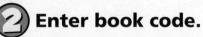